Also by Douglas Worth

Of Earth (1974)

INVISIBILITIES
Poems by Douglas Worth

Apple-wood Press   Cambridge

ACKNOWLEDGMENTS

For permission to reprint some of these poems, the author wishes to thank the editors of the following: Apple-wood Press, Creativities, Dark Horse, Longhouse, New American Poetry, (McGraw-Hill, 1973), Nitty-Gritty, 100 Flowers Anthology, People, Poems & Pictures, Prologue, The Alaska Review, The Colorado Quarterly, The Henniker Review, The Lamp in the Spine, The Little Magazine, The Little Review, The Logic of Poetry, (McGraw-Hill, 1974), The New Earth Review, New York Poetry, Triptych, Trout Poems, and Workshop.

"Crone" (originally entitled "Bell and Candle") reprinted from Prairie Schooner, copyright © 1968 by the University of Nebraska Press.

"Flashback" (originally entitled "The Four Ages") reprinted from The Massachusetts Review, copyright © 1966 by the Massachusetts Review, Inc.

"Orpheus, Turning" and "Breakthrough" forthcoming in Aspect.

162279

ISBN: 0-918222-01-X hardcover
ISBN: 0-918222-02-8 paperback

INVISIBILITIES

Fred

CONTENTS

"What is essential is invisible to the eye."

Saint-Exupéry, **The Little Prince**

QUEST

always
about to arrive
elsewhere
than this
obviousness, imagining
marvels unfolding
the sudden
transfiguring slant

surrounded
by the familiar
landscape of things as they are
where one might concede
at any point, finding oneself
in the present, eternally
flowering, withering moment, the fabulous
unredeemed here and now

POET

strange bird
the people do not love you
your eyes where
angels nest among roots

you go to work
you vote
you read the news

again
in mid-sentence, stepping down
from the curb, a stone
rolls aside, the air is a river
of wings, your pen runs blood

TOUCHSTONE

without wings, or wand, bright
banner of cause or state

to perceive

in acts and objects, common
as light, as dust

nimbus, essence, web

WORDS

you taste each
color, edge

even in those worn smooth
as pebbles, a muted
power
that still might

blaze suddenly
flowering
into song

CRAFT
(for Fred)

form gets the prize
the write-up, how the craft
skims, seamless
lines converge, clash, sweep
toward masterpiece
and the high finish
gleaming, the brilliant
success

but the guts, the juice driving
the honed edge into the deep
braced, kneeling, blinded, hands sliding
with brine, blood, odor of shipwreck
in the wind, rising
again and again, the sudden
uncontrollable shivering
grace of the god

SELF PORTRAIT: WRITING

Beginning in darkness
I see myself

obscurely
in the window

become with the light
the world.

WORLDS
(for William Bronk)

Being here
we go on as if
it makes sense

this precarious, wild
sometimes painfully
beautiful act

we perform
over and over, whirling
through space

of tearing down, building
from chaos, order
a home—

those before us, after us
tearing down, building
again

imperfect, fictions
all, yet part
of the one

that has made us
what we are
as if through us

the world is trying
to make sense
of itself.

PROGRESS
(for Alison and Roge)

Is that light at the end of the tunnel
getting brighter
as we grow used to the dark?

We seem to be moving
ahead, but who knows?
who would remember
days spun from pure sunlight and weather
the dance and the hunt
and the strange voice calling
from that obscure cavernous entrance?

Whom can we ask
when even our chromosomes seem bent on
consigning to apes, or to Eden, whatever
grace may have dimmed, then flickered out
behind?

EARLY NOMADIC ANIMAL ART

Innocent of the latest
city craze
they recast plundered bronze
to what they knew

the mountain lion
flattening to spring
the stag's dilated nostrils
sucking doom
were ornament enough
for warrior buckle
scabbard, stallion cheek.

Today, when what's most scoured of life
prevails
in the chic modern
galleries

pausing above
each lighted case, we feel
under three thousand years
of verdigris
the same hot shudder slide
from knotted shoulder blades
to tingling hooves.

THE MESSAGE OF THE SENOI
(for James Moore)

We find it hard to believe them
those tantalizing accounts
we come across now and then
waiting for trains or the dentist
of the Incas or some tribe
like the Senoi in Malay
still living obscurely among us
without locks or the need for locks
and no wars for centuries
and always treating each other
as what we call human beings
by which we really mean saints

but there they are, documented
in **National Geographic**
or **The Times Sunday Magazine**
and we have to accept them as fact
so we do, which raises the question
of who's gotten off the track
and if it's us what can we do
about it, right here and now?

Of course we'd like to believe
that we could live that way too
despite what we know about Nixon
and getting from day to day
and what became of Christ
and what our brothers did
that time to our favorite toy
just as we'd like to believe
in Scrooge on Christmas morning
or **Appalachian Spring**
the whole year round, but we can't.

So in the end we reject them
and not without despair
mixed with a sense of relief
because we had secretly tried
putting their message to work
carried it shyly around with us
for a while, like a charm that frayed
the lining of a pocket
until some crisis came up
and it found its way to a drawer
strewn with pamphlets on meditation
hope for the blind, and such
things as we meant to come back to
once the air cleared a bit

or if there had been no crisis
we thought about less and less
till one day, making a dash
against the light, we could feel it
along with some change and a token
we could have used, slipping away.

THE SUMMER HOUSE
(for Viki)

He never asked
preferring
not to know
why the church bell below his terrace
chimes the hours twice
leaving a timeless space
of silence in between—
the first few days
new to the country
he had thought it strange
that time upon these hills
should seem to stop

but hour circling hour
days, months, years
the fact became a welcome
ritual
part of the rhythm
of his laboring
pressed slowly on his mind
till it became symbolic
of a life
that might have been
conceived in Eden
once between a time.

Now, through the rich
late August afternoon,
a text, notebooks
a newspaper from home

spread on the table
where he sits at work,
he feels the year recede
the slanting light
upon him like a weight
indifferent
to all his years
have still to undertake.

A sudden bell breaks
inward on his thought,
another—vision blurs:
the warm green hills
caught in a flood
of light and music, rise:
above, circling
on weightless wings, a hawk
carves azure endlessly
till time itself
unravelling air and bone
must catch its breath.

                    Vesancy, France

VESANCY

mornings, the windows
are doors, opening
inward

the mind in that light
washed naked, we enter
as children

a landscape whose objects
in their first freshness
come nuzzling our senses

one after one
to be named

FLASHBACK
(for Mother and Dad)

the strawberries
that summer, lasted forever
and the apple trees always
blossoming, dropping and bending,
huge swallowtails gracefully
flitting from nets we flung

and the long evenings, voices
of grown-ups drifting in bursts
from the moonlit lawn
mysterious, muffled
as moth wings colliding, buzzing
against the screen

GUESTS IN EDEN
(for Ellen)

sun-lazing, mornings
looking out
from the high terrace
it is as if
one has not asked too much
has earned
these few weeks, guests in Eden

yarrow sloping to meadow
ash and oak
a village
patchwork of farmland rolling beyond
to a city, too distant to touch us
decorative,
in the sheltering mountains
mille fleurs walks

but a letter, in dreams
another world encroaching . . .

what they could see
from the rose-clouded fence:

the animals, flowering
antler, crest, and mane
opposed, proud, violent
slaughtering one another

slow-paced and courtly
the same creatures, caught
in the inextricable
pageant of desire—

inside them, countering
all that peace
the less and less containable need
to reach out and touch, to know
whatever is . . .

our own ambivalence, taking leave
of the dove-filled trees
the streams, endless windings
through bluebells and raspberries
suggesting what pain
they suffered, as they turned
to meet the unknown
dimly advancing fall

RETURN

The Times feels heavy, day
skids by on squealing rubber
nothing has changed
but flashes

inside us, stars
that still appear
so close our hands
might brush them away

flooding the subway, fields
where we lay and fed
each other's mouths ambrosial
wine and bread

STRAPHANGER

Half-curled
above some lady's shoulder
the nails chipped
blades of old tools
the skin indifferent
a hide for all weathers

it bears veins in a web
delicate as lace
for a lover
or the skeleton
of a child's ship, still drying
in a vise.

WAKING

a blue that burns
the edges clean
gold running the grain

at the window
a branch
from Van Eyck's hand

smoke winds
the sun shaft
tapestry

dreamwork
too delicate
to sustain

red-eyed
the morning
clears its throat

a savage
energy
grinds into gear

DEER CROSSING
(for Karen)

there
where we've put a road through
and put up a sign

we encounter
the problem

of our being
both in and out
of nature

indifferent
and responsible
to her laws

though for the most part we manage
to avoid it

sometimes at night
the blind eyes, the machine
interpenetrate

'THE SMALL NOUNS'
(for George Oppen)

bird
in the sense of wonder
and recognition

and therefore
an anguished
sense of oneself

alive, among fellow
creatures, precariously
acting and exposed

in a world
of flowering
metals, singing

bird
in the sense
of prayer

SNOWDROPS

exposing, this morning
white tips so fragile
they bruise in wind

do not mistake them

whose ancestors gauged
eons of granite
and harnessed the sun

DANNY, 2 WEEKS

lids fluttering still
wings in the milky
moonflower of sleep, sweet
baby, you're smiling
at the angels, as they say
and why not, I
still get up that way
now and again, myself

THE CHILDREN'S BOOKS

Cautioned implicitly
against that breed
of kindly beasts and boys
raised on love's sweet excess
he could not see, at dinner
when the talk began to sour
and throats went dry
and someone slammed a dish
and someone else's eyes
were a dead fish
and no one said a word
for half-an-hour

he blamed himself, his parents
then the books,
later regretted
the hyprocrisy
and planned a future free
of the absurd—
married, in love with her
clear ways and looks
he suffered the birth
of a new family
passing his old books on
without a word.

BOAT POND

leaf, paper cup, machine
moving together
through a world
of green

over wide water
dream prevails
the whole horizon blossoming
with sails

SLAP

mountainous, the ancient
tyranny of the big
as against the need, real need
for law . . . crumbling

my hand reaching out
to find you, afraid
which you took, as if a branch
of olive . . . gathering

lifting you, safe
safe, safe, little love, a wonder
any of us survives

SEA-CHALLENGER
(for Marc)

Knee-deep in swirling foam
lips curling, clenched fists raised
you watch the breakers glide
and build till they loom like walls
that towering pitch and plunge
crashing against your chest.

Little sea-challenger
sand caving under your feet
how can you stop the waves
that can wrestle oaks to the ground
as they slowly crush and grind
mountains to glittering dust?

But to take such a stance, to feel
muscle and bone and will
bracing, as shock after shock
you meet that relentless thrust
spray dazzling your eyes, on your tongue
the salt of life strong and sweet!

SCHOOLGIRL

who
so supple, coolwhite, curved
some swan
must have claimed her
mother, exploding
all fruit, her mouth opening
ripe, rape
as she ascends
the 3 o'clock bus with her friends

THE PACK

Raking jungles
from lenses, collars, greasy
metal-mouthed mugs spewing
Marlboro Country
pollution

they enter Annie's
like bad news, taking
over the counter, ordering
cokes, grinders to go with
ugly assurance

hunch on raw elbows, covering
exposure by snarling
at one another, eyeing
the waitress, screwing
around with the sugar, squeezing
the mustard and ketchup to obscene
ejaculations

paying in sullen
discomfort, grabbing their bags
change, extra straws and napkins, a pack
of adolescents, not at home
here, at school, or anywhere
moving on.

EAGLE

When the ungainly brood
are of an age

he leads them
up to thin bare boughs

and abandons them
to flop in the wind

hiding himself
on a low branch upstream

where for weeks unflinching
he watches the sky

for panic and hunger to toughen
their reluctant sinews

then drives them screaming
into their lives.

GROWN-UP

like when you find yourself
looking around and asking
'Who the fuck's in charge here?'
and it's you

SIGNAL

As she enters
the heads of all the men in the place
lift and turn

unthinking, fixed
in an expanding
silence

at the center of which
she moves and is held
is pierced.

When she sits down
and orders
her voice breaks something
like air
going out of a balloon

and the heads return
to their casual
sipping and munching, their papers
and talk.

No one says anything
about it
no one has to
or could

but something, a drop
of primordial juice has seeped through
the news of the day

and the tips of her breasts
stay stiffened, alert
as if awaiting
some further signal

as she pays
and snaps up her purse.

SKIN FLICK

because the alternative
is hard, is almost too much
the risk: pierced, swept off, sliding

to the verge of self, beyond, where
luminous, blossoming
no word for it: 'love,' 'I love you'
missing, the charged air flickering
the moment withering, leaving us
exposed, raw, shrinking
back, out
of the garden
of each other . . .

this
reduction, these bodies
consumers, anonymous
meat

THE GOD, THE GODDESS

1

Before them, blurred, distorted
is the image
of two lovers they've never seen before
who don't seem to know themselves
or each other either
as they hammer and gobble
one another's bodies
blindly, their flesh on the cheap film
stained by a light
that seems itself wounded, raw
until, in some bleak charade
of consummation
gravy of semen slithers
down her chin.

2

Before them, standing together
bathed in the light
of oil lamps, flickering
a deep blue-green
fragrance of forest
flowers around his neck,
he is dark, and radiant, fathomless
ocean, jewel, his flute resting
lightly in one hand, the other

clasping her
whose beauty is softer
more fluid, a river
of gold.

They begin to sing
of his flute, its infinite
tenderness, longing, power
searching the meadows, calling
compelling her,
the loveliness of her dancing
each gesture, glance
delicate and quick
as a lightning flash,
the dark and gold of their trembling
bodies flowing together
mingling, blurred.

3

One rises from the crowd
stands a moment, rocking
starts to weave
past faces turning along the aisle,
suddenly staggers, whirls, his eyes
glazed, a green glitter,
balances, whirls again
and, like some ancient
genius of the place
calling out darkly
to the god, the goddess,
stretches his arms wide
and begins to dance.

TO MY PENIS

Fellow poet, conspirator
furtively dreaming
through the days, dormantly
reticent, cloaked, constrained, shriveled
into yourself
or drawn out, sluggishly spouting
the usual garbage

hail!
I have seen you otherwise
revealed

inspired, mysteriously
rising to your full stature
swaying, inflamed, possessed
by your muse, the goddess
a vessel, brimmed
with the Word, ecstatic, shuddering forth
from your mouth, jet upon jet
the sacred fountain.

MUSE

When you come carelessly
naked from the shower
passing from room to room
shaking out your hair

what can I do
but follow

while something of that
cast-off radiance flows
gathers, and flows again
down the blank page.

TOUCHING

words fail
the body's clarity
what **are** we now?

coming
together
we fit

rolling apart
smoke lifts
to the ceiling

where the moon projects
a branch, the frame
of a window

WALK

beyond us, moments, woods
where neither could say
if the world disappeared or stood
revealed in its gold

but that wakening
seed in the heart
shed its mantle of clay

shivering, starlike, bloomed
'eternity in an hour'
blown away

SPRING AGAIN

Walking back to the cabin
the pond's edge black with tadpoles

we buried our faces in white
clusters of mountain laurel

skirting a ravaged sack of bones
spilling back slowly to marsh grass

stunned by a scarlet tanager
glistening from dense pine

like a fresh drop of blood.

ORPHEUS, TURNING

not out of doubt

to release her, both
no longer of either world

the blood ore
in his veins, her eyes flowering
diamonds, waiting for him

to turn and plunge blindly
into the alien
light

LOVERS

all of us
writhing, caught
in the world's embrace, each other's
dreams and shit on our hands

DA NANG

in the dream I would have done anything
to stay alive

face, our face, we have seen it
before, and now in living color, barbarous
face of the human
machine breaking down

walking through woods I thought
I am leaf, rock, in the wind
it is enough

it is not enough

NIGHTMARE

waking
to a world where things were
reversed

ourselves two-headed, lumbering
through landscapes
of children

terrified of what
our hands, monstrous
could and could not do

CHRISTMAS

the children
under the illumined tree

bombarded
scrambling out, shrieking
for us to see

our gifts
ablaze in their hands

OVER THERE

The chicken-necked farmer
turning
his sour fields

knows things
aren't going to get much better
either way.

Here, the newspapers
go on piling up
the dead

sifting, computing
faceless
averages

like the sports page
towards the end
of a dismal season

when nobody should have won
and by November nobody knows
who did.

PEACE WITH HONOR

eroded, cringing
inward
as we try
to strip war from us

what we had thought
a mask, turned
cancerous
skin

can we now settle
in our lives
for peace
without connection

honor
that rouge
of protocols, failing
love?

STAR MARKET

galaxies
of large, extra large
jumbo

dwarfed by sheer magnitude, one creeps
at the foot of some gargantuan
appetite

reaching out to what, bewildering
paradise of the latest
gods?

REPUBLIC

what had been conceived
as a land
ruled by the people
growing, becoming

confused
by size, sheer number
the machinery grinding, advancing
out of hand

lives mangled
the people receding, caught
in the relentless logic
of their own success

in the wake of empire
bands
of the saved, the eroded
going under, turning

inward, back
to the simple, eternal
light
in the Orient

DREAMERS

who ached beyond
mere drudgery of subsistence
urging the possible
a little further
than at first it had wanted to go

LINCOLN TO JFK

Does it bloom
in every dooryard, brother
lifting sweet petals to each shower
and after, fragrance so rich
when the clusters brush your cheek
it stuns the breath?

Or does that dream still lie
mutilated, wasted, torn
roots and leaves drifting
in another flood
of statesmen's rhetoric
and soldiers' blood?

THE TASK

one day the clear task
unfolding, dazzling, immense
vision piercing the heart
of a horizon so vast even death
would be a kind of success

then months, years of this slogging
through piled snow, leaves, where the path
keeps losing itself in brambles, and whatever
that voice up ahead is calling, it is not
the sea! the sea!

READING
(for Denise Levertov)

Activist, lover, oracle
each in turn
surfacing, taking up
weaving the complex
burden
of your song
from that beautiful
flawed
aging, ageless
human face

whatever else happens to you
whatever acts
of sanctioned atrocity
sear your heart's marrow, loves
in their juice and mystery bloom
and drift
clouding your window, angels
rise shimmering
from the ruins before you
on eternal wings

burning, keening, illumined
lightly
touching a hand to your hair
we know you
will never let us abandon
deny or absolve
the world you have seen
so deeply, dared
to sing for us
so well.

MICHELANGELO

a little man
disfigured
imagine

the beautiful people
in the parks, public gardens
crowded, at dusk

his dwarfish figure
among them, shouldering home
paint-spattered, searching each gesture

his room, the mirror avoided
before sleep the dim ceiling
swarming with gods

ELEGY
(for Rainer Maria Rilke)

Beginning, on your own
even as a child
you found words
playing hide-and-seek
with things.

Not so much alone
as elsewhere, out of touch
with the others at their games,
missing the ball
you leapt for the sun instead
sinking beyond the fingers
of the trees—
and you found words
that caught the fall
of things.

In class, when they asked for dates
of battles, kings
you gave them the circling
eagles behind time's eyes
and bared a glittering era
with a phrase—
for you found words
that stripped the rind
from things.

Drifting through the conventions
of the days and years,
mealtimes, jobs, fashions, cities
happened to you
though you had trouble remembering

directions, names, and the latest
news never took you
where you wanted to go—
but you found words
that sipped the juice
of things.

One day you sucked the heart
out of a rose;
once the deep singing
marrow from an oak;
one night a girl
burst on your tongue
like a burning seed—
you had found words
that plunged to the core
of things.

Unsatisfied, your thirst
for discovery grew so great,
abandoning earth, you soared
up to the dim cathedral
of the heavens;
advancing, star by star
you sensed the invisible
presence of awesome powers
pervading, ordering, binding
the universe,
and called them angels, beyond us
flowing in pure
unalterable perfection
as veins through alabaster
next to those

threading the softer white
of a woman's wrist—
and you found words
that bowed before the mystery
of things.

Chastened, you returned
to the familiar
seamless face of things,
letting them dwell and be
inside you, shining
more sweetly for their corrupt
mortality—leaf, wing, stone
transfigured, radiant, each
a little sun,
that had not been
and never would be again,
caught up by forces, flung
on some fathomless journey
blindly, each in its time
adding irrevocably
its tiny sum
to the infinite
flowing of eternity—
and you found words
that praised
the passing-in-everlastingness
of things.

One day they came, lamenting
that you had died
and bore away a shell
and were satisfied,

but you had left them the living
fruits of your eyes
for all who would come
and like you, reaching, try
the mingled tastes of earth
and paradise,
and gone on ahead—
and you found words
that were not words for things
translations, but things themselves
speaking their native tongues,
and became one with them
beginning again.

Vesancy—Muzot—Raron

OTHER

looms on the horizon, radiant
angel or demon
of infinite possibility advancing

till half-blinded, trembling, limbs aching
to turn, to reach out
new leaves

we stand gazing beyond
whatever we are
or were

BREAKTHROUGH

that shiver
and flood of wreckage
light, the blind
beak piercing the shell

FOUNTAIN

from dream, from circumstance, what we try
to make of ourselves—that fountain
in the cemetery, the ragged jet
splashing down to the basin, gathered
in a moving stillness, spilled over
clear threads twisting windblown
the chipped stone scattering beads

the art, the disappearing
act of life

CRONE

She can remember reading
when she was young
a poem about death's approach

how he'd come
bearing a little silver bell
and a low-fluttering candle

she forgets
what they were used for
but the image struck her as perfect—

all but gone
as she says, now he'd need thunder
and the sun.

2 LEAVES

whirling together
scattered
across the window's
blue

it could have been
monarchs, sparrows
it could have been
us

my parents checking out
old age homes

the kids tired
of wrestling

you and I
after sex

that moment
of completion, falling
away

the eyes blank
jelly
looking nowhere
at nothing
in nor out

TRANSFIGURATION
(for Val)

piecemeal, the world
is falling
in through the holes
of the body
filtered
by the mind and heart
down to that dark
dense core

which opens, or closes
in hunger, sated
nourished, battered
responding, avoiding

riots and roses, sparrows
Mozart, potatoes, murders
crabgrass and lovers

the debris
of days, rotting
scraps of information

sifting, dissolving

elephants, fashions, philosophers
toppling
whole cities crumbling
wars, generations, breakthroughs
pouring in
through the cracks

compressed
silting down

the weight of it
growing, the pressure
building

the small self struggling
to absorb, to escape

and there is no way
out

old civilizations
drifting, the dust, the dreams
of millennia
galaxies

relentlessly
pressing in

till it cannot be borne
or resisted
another minute
everything
collapses
caves in
goes black

black

black

no

something

is beginning
to happen
down there
in the dark

something

has cracked
a crust
seed
spark
flickering
deep
at the crux

is lifting
unfolding
frail
petal-feathers
of light

look

it is the world
transfigured, rising
a new, fragrant
jewel, singing
star